WHY DID GRANDPA CRY?

WRITTEN BY:
CATHY WERLING

ILLUSTRATED BY:
JACK BOHM

PUBLISHED BY:

Lowell Milken Center
FOR *Unsung Heroes*

© 2017 LOWELL MILKEN CENTER FOR UNSUNG HEROES
ALL RIGHTS RESERVED

Jennifer couldn't believe that the day was finally here! She was so excited! Her grandpa was coming to speak to the students at her school. She had listened to some of his talks before and knew how much people liked his story.

One thing she did know, though, was that Grandpa would definitely cry. He always did that when he gave his talks, and she often wondered what made him cry. What would the other kids think when they saw his tears? Would they think it was strange, or would they think it was special?

Jennifer's grandpa was Ken Reinhardt. People called him an "unsung hero," a person who did something very important but not many people knew about it. They said he had been very brave when he was in high school. She had heard him tell his story before and did think he had done something that would be very hard to do. She was anxious to listen to him tell his story again and to have her friends and teachers hear it.

Now it was finally time! Everyone was in the auditorium, and her grandpa was up on the stage. The principal introduced him, and everybody started clapping as he stood up to talk.

Jennifer heard her grandpa's voice, and he was talking about his granddaughter who went to this school. The kids and teachers turned to look at her - it made her feel a little funny, but also very proud!

The auditorium got very quiet as Grandpa began to tell his story.......

"I am sure you can all remember the first day you started classes in this school, or the first day you walked into a new classroom at the beginning of the year. It might have been exciting, maybe a little scary. I am going to tell you about a classmate of mine who will never forget the first day she walked into our high school in Little Rock, Arkansas."

"She was very scared, and rightly so. Instead of laughing and talking with friends as she walked up the sidewalk to the school, she was walking alone. Many people and other students were standing on each side of her and walking behind her. They were yelling at her in very mean ways and calling her names. Many were telling her to go home, and some were even spitting on her!"

"Her name was Elizabeth Eckford, and she was one of nine black students coming to Little Rock Central High School for the first time. You see, before that year of 1957, our school was only for white students. Black students had to go to their own schools."

"Things were changing, though, and a new law had passed in our country. The law said that black and white students should be able to go to the same schools. My family and I agreed with that law. I was raised to believe all people were important and should be treated the same."

"Many white families in Little Rock didn't like that law and continued to treat black people as if they were not as good as whites. The governor of Arkansas was one who felt that way, and he had soldiers block the black students from going to school that first day."

"Elizabeth and the eight other black students had to wait to start school. Many days later, the President of the United States sent more soldiers to walk with the nine black students and keep them safe as they went into the school."

"The soldiers had to stay for the whole school year. They stood guard as the nine students walked to their classrooms and in the halls because there were so many white students who treated them in awful ways."

"I couldn't imagine how bad it had to feel to be treated like Elizabeth was. When I walked into my speech class that year, I saw Elizabeth sitting all alone in a corner desk. No one was talking to her, and many were giving her mean looks."

"I knew that was not right, so I sat down beside her. As I talked with her, I asked if there was anything I could do to help her. I always tried to treat her with kindness and respect, just as I believed all people should be treated."

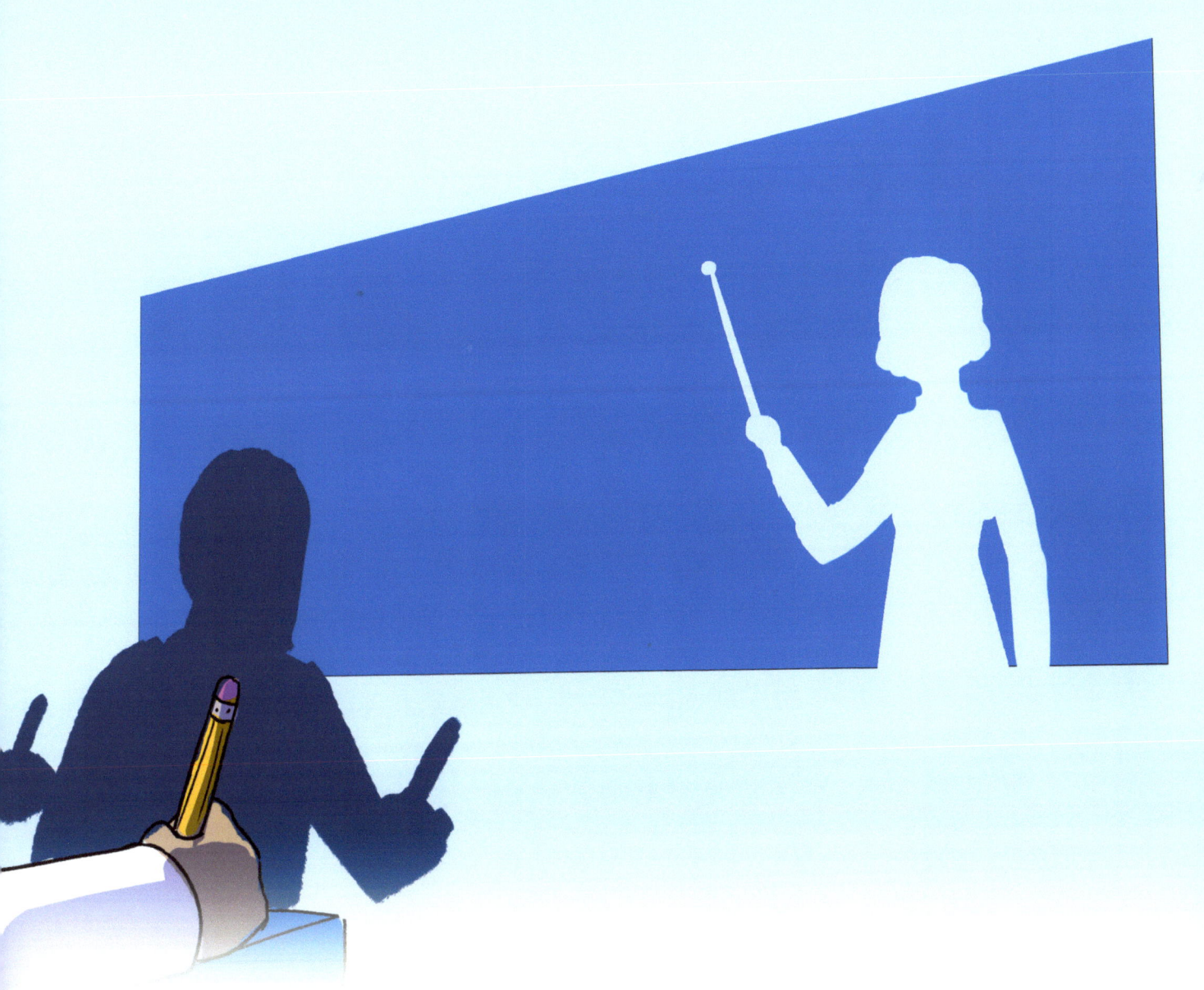

"Another girl in our class, Ann Williams, felt the same way that I did. She was also kind to Elizabeth and talked to her in class."

"The sad thing is that there were not many others that felt like Ann and I did. Most of the white students continued to treat Elizabeth and the eight other black students in very hateful ways. They refused to talk to them or sit by them. Sometimes the white students completely ignored the black students, acting as if they were not even there. Worse than that, they said and did mean and hurtful things to them."

"I got to know most of the nine black students at Central High School that year. They really were nice people, and I enjoyed talking to them and sharing time with them at school. I ate lunch with some of them, sat with them in class, and walked with them in the hall."

Because of the time I spent with those nine students, though, I, too, was treated in some pretty horrible ways. Many of my white classmates called me awful names. I was even shoved and punched by some, and there were threats that bad things would happen to me and my family."

"It wasn't an easy time - in fact, it was a scary time! I knew I was doing the right thing, though. I couldn't imagine being unkind to my black classmates. Standing up for what was right was something I learned from my family, and treating every person as special and important was the only choice I would consider."

"In fact, 40 years passed before the day I got a phone call from some Kansas students that wanted to know if I remembered Elizabeth Eckford. They told me they were studying about the year I graduated from Central High School and were doing a history project about an unsung hero. They said they had talked to Elizabeth, and she told them how hard it had been for her. They asked if there had been any white students who had been kind to her, and right away, she had said two names, 'Ken and Ann.'"

"She was talking about Ann Williams and me, Ken Reinhardt! After 40 years, Elizabeth still remembered our names and said we had been the ones who had made her feel better during one of the hardest times in her life. The students from Kansas said that Ann and I were heroes in the eyes of Elizabeth! How could we be heroes? We were just doing what we thought was right, what our parents had taught us to do."

As he finished his story, Jennifer's grandpa paused before sharing some important words with the students listening to him, "Boys and girls, that is why I am here talking to you today... to talk about heroes and being a person that makes a difference in someone's life, even when it isn't easy. Think about a boy or girl that you have seen sitting alone at lunch, with no one to talk to. Are there some kids that others make fun of because of the way they dress or the way they talk? Is there a child you know who never gets picked for games or always plays at recess alone? How would it feel to be one of those children?"

"What could you do to make a difference for them, to bring a smile to their faces and some joy to their hearts? Will they remember you as a 'hero' or as 'someone who was hurtful?' What will they say about you in the years to come? That is what I hope you will think about today."

Those last words really made Jennifer think. A new girl had come to Jennifer's class yesterday. Her name was Ling, and she did not speak English. Jennifer had seen Ling swinging by herself at recess, and she'd thought about trying to talk to her, but Jennifer's friends had wanted Jennifer to play with them, so she forgot about Ling.

How must it have felt to be all alone like Ling in a new school? Jennifer felt her cheeks getting wet, as tears fell from her eyes.

That is when Jennifer realized her grandpa was sitting down on the stage, and people were clapping for him as he finished his talk. She also realized that she wasn't the only one with tears on her cheeks. She saw many kids and teachers, too, wiping away tears from their eyes.

She hadn't even looked to see if Grandpa was crying, but it was okay if he was. Now, she knew why he cried. She felt it in her heart, just as she knew he felt it in his. Those tears meant that he cared. They were a mixture of sadness for the hurt that Elizabeth had suffered, and the joy that came from knowing his actions had brought some happiness to her life...

Jennifer wanted to be that kind of hero, too.

Unsung Hero Ken Reinhardt
True Stories That Shaped His Life and Actions

Ken and his family lived in Jonesboro, Arkansas during Ken's 7th through 10th grade years in school. The only movie theatre in town had a divided balcony. Black people could only sit on one side of the balcony and never on the main floor. The partition in the balcony was about three feet high, with metal rails that were another foot or two higher. Ken had a friend who was black, and when they went to the show, they would sit next to each other on either side of the dividing partition so they could visit.

Ken lived the first eight years of his life in Memphis, Tennessee. Most of that time, he and his family lived with his grandmother, Mimi. She had a black maid named Mary Lee, who was like another grandmother to Ken. She fed him, bathed him, spanked him, and loved him. One of Ken's favorite breakfasts prepared by Mary Lee was a scrambled egg sandwich loaded with ketchup.

Mary Lee would go to the store several times a week, pulling Ken along in his wagon. On one occasion, as they returned from the store, Mary Lee gave little Ken a spanking. A neighbor came running out of her house and yelled, "Don't you be spanking that white boy!". Upon hearing that, Ken yelled back, "She's my Mary Lee and she can spank me if she wants to!"

Mary Lee came every morning by bus and went home the same way. She was always treated as a member of the family. Even after Ken and his family moved away from Memphis, he and his two siblings would spend a week or two with Mimi each summer. Mary Lee still came to work for Mimi and never failed to spoil the children.

Over the years, as all of these things came to light, it was Ken's wife who helped him to understand the powerful influence Mary Lee had on his view of others, no matter the color of their skin.

Ken grew up in a home that took its faith and its church very seriously. He never heard a racial put-down in his home, and the value of people was always understood. What happened to the Little Rock Nine was a shock to Ken. He thought he understood prejudice, but he didn't understand the extreme hatred he witnessed. What was done to the Little Rock Nine was the kind of bullying that causes lifelong problems for those who experience it. Ken never expected the mean-spirited reaction to his simple gesture of friendship. The first reaction he received was from sitting down at lunch with Jefferson Thomas and shaking his hand. Ken was surprised the next day when several of his "friends" shoved him to the floor in gym class and warned him not to spend time with the nine black students.

www.ingramcontent.com/pod-product-compliance
Lightning Source LLC
Chambersburg PA
CBHW041126300426
44113CB00002B/71